New Testament Stories

Published by
The Church of Jesus Christ of Latter-day Saints
Salt Lake City, Utah

Contents

Sources

Some of the information in this book is taken from the nonscriptural sources cited below.

Bible Dictionary in the Latter-day Saint edition of the King James Version of the Bible (1979)

James E. Talmage, *Jesus the Christ,* 3rd edition (1916)

Teachings of the Prophet Joseph Smith, sel. Joseph Fielding Smith (1976)

To the Reader

New Testament Stories has been written especially for you. These stories are taken from a book that is sacred. As you read these stories, remember they are about real people who lived long ago.

Read the stories over and over until you know them well. You will also want to read them from the Bible. Under most of the pictures, you will see references that tell you where to find that story in the Bible or other books. Have your father, mother, teacher, or a friend help you find the story in the scriptures.

If you do not know what a word means, look it up in the "Words to Know" section at the back of the book. If you want to learn more about a place, look it up in the "Places to Know" section. If you do not know who a person is, look him or her up in the "People to Know" section. This book also has a section with photographs of places in the Holy Land and a New Testament time line.

To Parents and Teachers

This book can help you teach the scriptures. Use the "Words to Know," "Places to Know," and "People to Know" sections to help children become familiar with words, people, and places in this book. Other helps in this book include maps, photographs, and a time line.

As you teach, share your testimony of the Bible. Encourage those you teach to prayerfully seek their own testimonies of the scriptures and of the Savior, Jesus Christ. The understanding of those you teach will grow even greater as you read them their favorite stories from the Bible itself.

Our Heavenly Father's Plan

We lived in heaven with Heavenly Father before we came to earth. We are His spirit children and had spirit bodies. We loved Him, and He loved us.

Teachings of the Prophet Joseph Smith, *354*

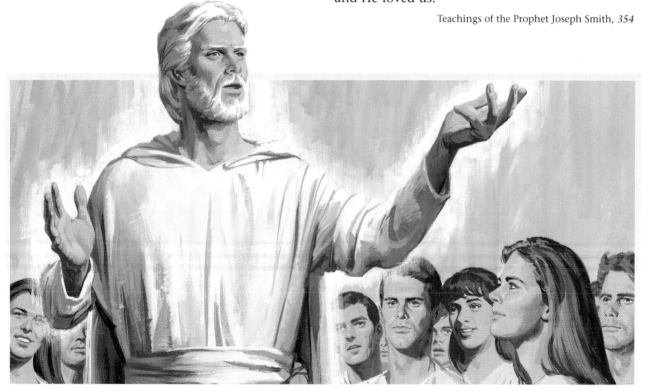

Heavenly Father taught us about His plan for us. It is called the plan of salvation. If we follow His plan, we can become like Heavenly Father. The plan was for us to come to earth and have bodies of flesh and blood. We would be tested to see if we would choose to obey God's commandments.

Abraham 3:24–25

The plan of salvation provides a way for us to live with Heavenly Father again. We would need to keep the commandments. But we would also need help. We would need to have our sins taken away, and we would need resurrected bodies. Because we cannot take away our own sins or resurrect our own bodies, we needed a Savior to do this for us.

2 Nephi 2:5–9

Heavenly Father chose Jesus Christ to be our Savior. Jesus loved Heavenly Father. Jesus also loved us. He agreed to come to earth to show us how to be righteous. He would provide the way for all of us to be saved. He agreed to suffer for our sins. He would also die and be resurrected so we would be resurrected too.

2 Nephi 2:8–9; Moses 4:1–2

Satan also wanted to be our savior. But he did not love Heavenly Father. He did not love us. He wanted to change Heavenly Father's plan so that he would have Heavenly Father's power and glory.

Moses 4:1–2

Some of Heavenly Father's spirit children chose to follow Satan. This made Heavenly Father very sad. He made Satan and his followers leave heaven. Satan is the devil. He and the spirits who followed him want us to sin.

Moses 4:3–4

Heavenly Father told Jesus to make an earth for us. Jesus did. He made the sun, the moon, and the stars. He put plants and animals on the earth. Now we had an earth to come to where we would have bodies of flesh and blood.

Hebrews 1:2; Mosiah 3:8; Abraham 4

Many people come to live on earth. Some of them choose to obey God's commandments; some do not. The ancient prophets taught the people about Heavenly Father's plan and about Jesus Christ.

2 Nephi 2:19–21; Jacob 7:10–11; Moses 5:13–15

The prophets said Jesus's father would be Heavenly Father. His mother would be a very good woman named Mary. He would be born in Bethlehem.

Isaiah 7:14; Micah 5:2; 1 Nephi 11:18–21; Alma 7:10

The prophets said that many people would not believe that Jesus was the Savior. He would look like other people and not be rich. Many people would hate Him.

Isaiah 53:2–3

The prophets also told about John the Baptist. He would come before Jesus to tell the people about Him. John would baptize Jesus.

Isaiah 40:3; Matthew 3:1–3; 1 Nephi 10:7–10; 11:27

The prophets said that Jesus would be kind and perform many miracles. Before He died, Jesus would suffer for the sins of all people so they would not have to suffer if they would repent.

Mosiah 3:5–8; Doctrine and Covenants 19:16–18

Many prophets knew that Jesus Christ, our Savior, would be crucified. He would be nailed to a wooden cross and give His life for us.

John 3:14–15; Mosiah 15:7–9

After three days, He would be resurrected. His spirit would come back into His body. Because Jesus would die and be resurrected, we would all be resurrected too.

Isaiah 25:8; 1 Corinthians 15:22; 2 Nephi 2:8; Alma 33:21–22

The New Testament shows that the words of the prophets are true. It is the story of Jesus Christ and His Apostles. They lived in the Holy Land.

Many of the people who lived there were called Jews. The Romans had captured the Holy Land, and they ruled over the Jews.

CHAPTER 1

Elisabeth and Zacharias

Zacharias and his wife, Elisabeth, were Jews who lived near Jerusalem. They obeyed God's commandments. For many years they prayed to have a baby. When they were old, they still had no children.

Luke 1:5–7, 13

Zacharias was a priest in the temple. One day an angel named Gabriel came to him. Gabriel said that God would answer Zacharias and Elisabeth's prayers. They would have a baby. Gabriel said they should name the baby John.

Luke 1:8–13, 19

Gabriel said that John would be a righteous
prophet of God. He would teach people about
Jesus Christ.

Luke 1:15–17

Zacharias did not believe the angel. Elisabeth was
too old to have a baby. Gabriel said that because
he did not believe what God had promised,

Zacharias would not be able to talk until John was
born.

Luke 1:18–20

CHAPTER 2

Mary and the Angel

Mary and Joseph lived in Nazareth. They were very good people. They loved each other and were going to be married.

Luke 1:26–27

One day the angel Gabriel came to Mary. He told Mary that God would bless her.

Luke 1:26, 28–30

Gabriel told Mary that she would be the mother
of the Son of God. His name would be Jesus, and
He would be the King of all righteous people.

Luke 1:31–33

Mary said that she would obey Heavenly Father
and be the mother of Jesus.

Luke 1:34–35, 38; 1 Nephi 11:18–21

CHAPTER 3

John the Baptist Is Born

The angel Gabriel told Mary that Elisabeth was also going to have a baby boy. Mary and Elisabeth were relatives.

Luke 1:36–37

Mary went to visit Elisabeth. The Holy Ghost told Elisabeth that Mary would be the mother of Jesus Christ. Mary and Elisabeth thanked God for blessing them. Mary stayed with Elisabeth for about three months. Then Mary went home to Nazareth.

Luke 1:39–56

Elisabeth's son was born. Her friends and family were happy. They thought that the baby should have the same name as his father, Zacharias. But Elisabeth said that his name should be John. Everyone was surprised.

Luke 1:57–61

The people asked Zacharias what the baby's name should be. Zacharias still could not talk, so he wrote, "His name is John."

Luke 1:62–63

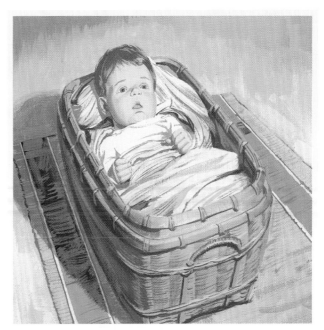

Then Zacharias was able to speak again. He was filled with the Holy Ghost. He told the people that Jesus Christ would soon be born and that John would prepare the people for Him.

Luke 1:64, 67–69, 76

John grew up to become a great prophet. He taught people about Jesus Christ.

Luke 1:67, 76–80

11

CHAPTER 4

Joseph and the Angel

Joseph was a good and kind man. He and Mary were to be married. When he learned that Mary was going to have a baby, he did not know what to do. Because the baby was not his child, he thought he should not marry her.

Matthew 1:18–19

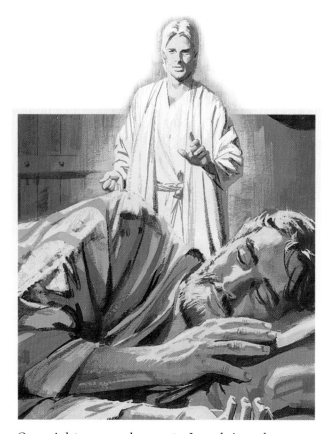

One night an angel came to Joseph in a dream and told him that Mary's baby was the Son of God. The angel told Joseph to marry Mary and to name her baby Jesus. Jesus was to be the Savior of the world.

Matthew 1:20–21

Joseph obeyed the angel and married Mary.

Matthew 1:24–25

CHAPTER 5

Jesus Christ Is Born

The Roman emperor made a law that everyone must pay taxes. Joseph and Mary lived in Nazareth. They had to go 65 miles (105 km) to Bethlehem to pay their taxes.

Luke 2:1–5

It was not easy for Mary to travel to Bethlehem. Her baby would soon be born.

Luke 2:4–5

When Joseph and Mary arrived in Bethlehem, all the rooms were filled with people. Mary and Joseph had to stay in a stable. A stable is a place where animals are kept.

Luke 2:6–7

There the baby was born. Mary wrapped Him in
cloth and laid Him in a manger. Joseph and Mary
named the baby Jesus.

Luke 2:7, 21

On the night Jesus was born, shepherds were taking care of their sheep in the fields near Bethlehem. An angel came to them. The shepherds were afraid.

Luke 2:8–9

The angel told them not to be afraid. He had wonderful news: The Savior, Jesus Christ, was born in Bethlehem. They would find Him lying in a manger.

Luke 2:10–12

The shepherds went to Bethlehem, where they saw the baby Jesus.

Luke 2:15–16

The shepherds were happy to see the Savior. They told other people about all they had heard and seen.

Luke 2:17, 20

15

CHAPTER 6

Presentation at the Temple

When Jesus was just a few weeks old, His parents brought Him to Jerusalem to present Him at the temple.

Luke 2:22

Simeon, a righteous man who lived in Jerusalem, was at the temple. The Holy Ghost told him he would see Christ before he died.

Luke 2:25–26

Simeon saw the baby Jesus at the temple. He held Him in his arms and praised God.

Luke 2:27–29

Simeon said that the child would bring salvation to all people. Joseph and Mary marvelled at what he said.

Luke 2:30–33

A widow named Anna also saw Jesus and knew who He was. She gave thanks and told many people about Him.

Luke 2:36–38

CHAPTER 7

The Wise Men

Some wise men lived in another land. They knew what the prophets had said about the birth of Jesus. When they saw a new star in the sky, they knew that a new king had been born.

Matthew 2:1–2

The Wise Men went to see Herod, a king of the Jews, in Jerusalem. They asked him where the new king was. Herod told them to look in Bethlehem. When they found the baby they were to come back and tell Herod.

Matthew 2:1–2, 8

The Wise Men went to Bethlehem and found Jesus. They worshipped Him and gave Him gifts. They were told in a dream not to go back to Jerusalem and tell Herod where the baby was. They didn't.

Matthew 2:11–12

CHAPTER 8

Wicked King Herod

The Wise Men had told Herod that Jesus would be king. Herod wanted to be the only king. He told his soldiers to kill all the babies in Bethlehem and nearby places.

Matthew 2:3, 13, 16

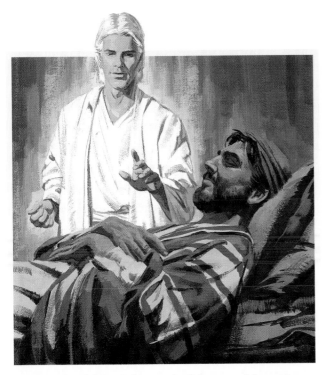

An angel told Joseph to take Mary and Jesus to Egypt, a country far from Bethlehem. Herod would not look for Jesus there.

Matthew 2:13

Joseph obeyed. He and Mary and Jesus were in Egypt when Herod's soldiers killed all the babies in Bethlehem and nearby places.

Matthew 2:14, 16

After King Herod died, an angel told Joseph to
take Jesus and Mary home. Joseph took them to
Nazareth, where Jesus was safe.

Matthew 2:19–21, 23

20

CHAPTER 9

The Boy Jesus

Jesus grew up in the city of Nazareth. He learned many things and became "strong in spirit, . . . and the grace of God was upon him."

Luke 2:39–40

When Jesus was 12, He went with Joseph and Mary in a group of people to a celebration in Jerusalem. They were there for several days.

Luke 2:41–43

When Joseph and Mary left for home, they thought that Jesus was walking back to Nazareth with His friends. But Jesus had stayed in Jerusalem.

Luke 2:43–44

When Joseph and Mary looked for Jesus, they could not find Him. No one in their group had seen Him. So Joseph and Mary went back to Jerusalem. They looked for Jesus for three days. They were very sad.

Luke 2:44–46

At last they found Jesus in the temple, talking with some teachers. He was answering their questions. The teachers were surprised at how much Jesus knew.

Luke 2:46–47 (see footnote 46c)

23

Mary told Jesus that she and Joseph had been worried about Him. Jesus replied that He was doing His Father's work—God's work. Joseph and Mary did not understand.

Luke 2:48–50

Jesus went home to Nazareth with Joseph and Mary and obeyed them.

Luke 2:51

Jesus learned more and more about His Heavenly Father's work.

Luke 2:52

He grew tall and strong.

Luke 2:52

People loved Him. He did what God wanted Him to do.

Luke 2:52

God loved Him.

Luke 2:52

CHAPTER 10

Jesus Is Baptized

John lived in the desert for many years. He wore clothes made of camel's hair, and he ate honey and locusts. People came from the cities to hear him teach. He was known as John the Baptist.

Matthew 3:1–5

John the Baptist taught the people about Jesus Christ. He told them to repent of their sins and be baptized. John baptized those who repented of their sins.

Matthew 3:2–3, 5–6

The people asked John the Baptist how to live better lives. He told them to share with the poor, tell the truth, and be fair to others. He said that Jesus Christ would soon come. Jesus would give them the gift of the Holy Ghost.

Matthew 3:2, 11–12; Luke 3:10–14

One day when John the Baptist was baptizing people in the Jordan River, Jesus Christ came to him. He asked John to baptize Him.

John knew that Jesus had always obeyed God's commandments and did not need to repent. John thought that Jesus did not need to be baptized.

Matthew 3:13–15; 2 Nephi 31:5–7

But God had commanded all people to be baptized, so Jesus told John to baptize Him.

Jesus set an example for us by obeying God's commandment to be baptized.

Matthew 3:16; 2 Nephi 31:7–9

When Jesus came up out of the water, the Holy Ghost came to Him. God spoke from heaven, saying, "This is my beloved Son, in whom I am well pleased." John the Baptist also testified that Jesus was the Son of God.

Matthew 3:16–17; John 1:33–36; Jesus the Christ, 150

CHAPTER 11

Jesus Is Tempted

Jesus went into the wilderness to be with God. The Savior talked with Heavenly Father. He did not eat anything for 40 days because He was fasting.

Matthew 4:1–2 (see footnotes 1b and 2c); Luke 4:1–2 (see footnote 2a)

The devil came and tempted Jesus to prove that He was the Son of God. First, he told Jesus to change some rocks into bread. Jesus was hungry, but He knew that He should use His power only to help other people. He did not do what the devil said.

Matthew 4:2–4; Jesus the Christ, 128–29

Next the Holy Ghost took Jesus to a high place on the temple. The devil tempted Jesus a second time, telling Him to jump off the temple wall. The devil said that if Jesus was the Son of God, the angels would not let Him be hurt. Jesus did not jump. He knew that it would be wrong to use His sacred powers in this way.

Matthew 4:5–7 (see footnotes 5a and 6a)

Then the Holy Ghost took Jesus to the top of a mountain. He showed Jesus all the kingdoms and treasures of the world. The devil told Jesus that He could have all these things if He would obey him. Jesus said He would only obey Heavenly Father. He told the devil to go away. The devil left. Angels came and blessed Jesus. Jesus was ready to begin His work.

Matthew 4:8–11 (see footnotes 8a and 9a)

CHAPTER 12

The Wedding in Cana

Jesus Christ and His disciples attended a wedding feast in Cana. Mary, Jesus's mother, was there. She told Jesus that there was no more wine for the guests.

John 2:1–3

Jesus respected and loved His mother. He asked her what she wanted Him to do.

John 2:4 (see footnote 4a)

Mary told the servants at the wedding to do whatever Jesus told them to do.

John 2:5

Jesus told the servants to fill six large stone jars with water. Each jar held between 18 and 27 gallons (68 and 102 liters). He then turned the water into wine.

John 2:6–7

He told the servants to take wine from the jars and serve it to the ruler of the feast.

John 2:8

The ruler of the feast was surprised when he drank the wine. The best wine was usually served at the beginning of a feast. But this time, the best wine was served last.

John 2:9–10

This is the first recorded miracle that Jesus performed during His life on earth. He did it to help His mother. It also helped strengthen the faith of His disciples.

John 2:11

33

CHAPTER 13

Jesus and His Heavenly Father's House

Jesus went to the temple in Jerusalem. Many people were there to make a sacrifice by killing an animal and burning it on an altar. The sacrifice helped people think about the Savior, who would sacrifice Himself by suffering and dying for them.

Leviticus 1:3–9; John 2:13; Moses 5:5–7

Some people did not have an animal to sacrifice. People sold animals to them in the temple. The sellers wanted to make a lot of money. They did not think about God.

John 2:14

Jesus saw the people selling animals in the temple. He said that the temple was Heavenly Father's house, a holy place. He said people should not buy or sell things there.

John 2:16

Jesus made a whip, overturned the tables, threw the money on the floor, and made the sellers leave the temple. He would not let them do wicked things in Heavenly Father's house.

John 2:15–16

CHAPTER 14

Nicodemus

Nicodemus belonged to a group of Jews called Pharisees. He was also a ruler of the Jews. Many Pharisees did not believe that Jesus Christ was sent by God. But Nicodemus believed because of the miracles Jesus did.

John 3:1–2

Nicodemus came to talk with the Savior one night. Jesus told him that no one could enter the kingdom of God without being born again.

John 3:2–3

Nicodemus did not understand. How could a person be born again? The Savior explained that He was talking about spiritual things. To be born again, a person must be baptized in water and receive the Holy Ghost.

John 3:4–7

Jesus explained that He had been sent to earth to help us all return to Heavenly Father. He said that He would suffer for our sins and die on a cross so that we could have eternal life.

John 3:12–17

He said that we need to believe in Him and choose the right. If we do what is right, we will live forever in the kingdom of God.

John 3:18–21

37

CHAPTER 15

The Woman at the Well

J esus left Jerusalem to go into Galilee. He traveled through Samaria and came to a well.

John 4:3–6

He was tired, and He rested by the well. A Samaritan woman came to get some water. Jesus asked her to give Him a drink.

John 4:6–7

Since Jews usually did not talk with Samaritans, the woman was surprised.

John 4:9

Jesus told the woman that He could give her a kind of water that would cause her never to thirst again. He explained that He was the Savior. The water He could give her was the "living water" of eternal life.

John 4:10, 13–15, 25–26

The woman went to the city and told many people about Jesus. They went to the well and listened to Jesus themselves. Many of them believed His words.

John 4:28–30, 39–42

CHAPTER 16

The Leader's Son

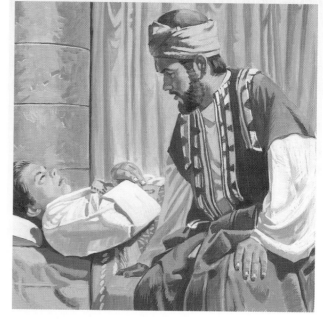

A leader of the Jewish people had a son who was very sick. Everyone thought that his son would soon die.

John 4:46–47

The man left his son at home and traveled many miles to the city of Cana. There he found Jesus.

John 4:47

The man asked the Savior to come and heal his son. Jesus told him that his son would be healed. The man believed Jesus, and he started for home.

John 4:47–50

His servants came to meet him. They told him that his son was getting better and would live. He asked them when his son had begun to get well.

They told him. It was at the same time Jesus had said that the son would be healed.

John 4:51–53

The man knew that Jesus Christ had healed his son. He and all his family believed in the Savior.

John 4:53

CHAPTER 17

Angry People in Nazareth

Jesus went to Nazareth, the city where He had grown up.

Luke 4:16

Jesus went to a synagogue, a building where Jews go to church. He stood up and read from the scriptures. He read the words of the prophet Isaiah. Isaiah had said that the Savior would come to earth and help all people.

Luke 4:16–19

When Jesus closed the scriptures and sat down, the people all looked at Him.

Luke 4:20

Jesus said that Isaiah's words were about Him—that He was the Savior. The people were amazed at His words. They said, "Is not this Joseph's son?" They did not believe that Jesus was the Son of God.

Luke 4:21–22

The Savior knew what they were thinking. They wanted Him to perform a miracle. But Jesus told them that He would not do miracles for them because they did not have faith in Him.

Luke 4:23–27

This made the people angry. They took Jesus to the top of a hill and wanted to throw Him off it.

Luke 4:28–29

Jesus escaped from them and went to another city.

Luke 4:30–31

CHAPTER 18

Jesus Chooses His Apostles

One day Jesus taught people from a boat on the shore of the Sea of Galilee. The boat belonged to a man named Peter.

Luke 5:1–3

Peter and his friends had fished all night without catching any fish. After Jesus finished teaching, He told Peter to take the boat into deep water.

Then He told Peter and his friends to put their fishing nets into the water.

Luke 5:4–5

They caught so many fish that their nets began to break.

Luke 5:6

Peter called to his friends in another boat to come and help. The fish filled both boats so full that they began to sink.

Luke 5:7

Peter and his friends were amazed. They knew that Jesus Christ had made this happen.

Luke 5:8–9

Peter knelt by the Savior's feet. He said that he was not worthy to be near Jesus. Jesus told Peter not to be afraid.

Luke 5:8–10

45

Two of Peter's friends, James and John, were brothers. Jesus told Peter, James, and John to follow Him and become "fishers of men." The men left everything they had and went with Jesus. The Savior also asked other men to follow Him.

Matthew 4:18–22; 9:9; Luke 5:10–11; John 1:35–51

Jesus chose twelve Apostles to lead His Church. He prayed all night so that He could choose the right men. The next morning He chose and ordained twelve men, giving them the priesthood and the authority to be Apostles.

Mark 3:14; Luke 6:12–16; John 15:16

The Apostles traveled to many cities. They taught the gospel and healed people. They returned to tell Jesus what they had done.

Mark 6:30; Luke 9:1–6, 10

CHAPTER 19

The Sermon on the Mount

One day Jesus taught His disciples the gospel on a mountainside by the Sea of Galilee.

Matthew 5:1

He told them how to live so they could be happy and live with Heavenly Father again. The things He taught them can make us happy too.

Matthew 5–7

Jesus said we should be gentle, patient, and willing to obey Heavenly Father.

Matthew 5:5

We should try as hard as we can to be righteous.

Matthew 5:6

We should forgive people who hurt us or make us feel bad. If we forgive them, Heavenly Father will forgive us.

Matthew 5:7

We should be peacemakers, love other people, and help everyone to love each other.

Matthew 5:9

We should not be afraid to tell people about the gospel or show them that we love Heavenly Father. When other people see us do good, it will help them believe in God too.

Matthew 5:14–16

We should always keep our promises.

Matthew 5:33–37

And just as we want others to be kind to us, we should be kind to them.

Matthew 7:12

Jesus said that if we do these things, we will be happy, Heavenly Father will bless us, and we will live with Him again.

Matthew 5:2–12

CHAPTER 20

Jesus Teaches about Prayer

Jesus taught His disciples how to pray. He said that some people pray only so others will see them praying. Jesus taught that we should say our personal prayers where we can be alone, if possible.

Matthew 6:5–6

He said that some people say the same words over and over when they pray. They do not really think about what they are saying. Jesus said that we should pray sincerely for what we need.

Matthew 6:7–8

The Savior said a prayer to show His disciples how to pray. He began by saying, "Our Father . . . in heaven." He praised Heavenly Father and then asked Him for help. He said "amen" at the end of His prayer. Later, Jesus told His disciples to pray to the Father in His name. He promised that Heavenly Father would answer their prayers.

Matthew 6:9–13; 21:22; John 16:23

CHAPTER 21

Jesus Commands the Winds and the Waves

Jesus and His disciples were in a boat on the Sea of Galilee. Jesus fell asleep. The wind began to blow very hard, and the waves were filling the boat with water. The disciples were afraid that it would sink. They woke Jesus and asked Him to help.

Luke 8:22–24

The Savior commanded the wind to stop blowing and the waves to go down. The wind stopped, and the sea became calm.

Luke 8:24

Jesus asked the disciples why they were afraid. He said that they should have more faith. They wondered what kind of man could command even the wind and the sea.

Mark 4:40; Luke 8:25

CHAPTER 22

The Man with the Evil Spirits

A man who lived in a cemetery by the Sea of Galilee had an evil spirit in him that made him act wild. People bound him with chains to control him, but he broke the chains.

Mark 5:1–4

The man spent all day and night in the mountains and caves. He cried all the time and cut himself with stones.

Mark 5:5

One day Jesus and His disciples crossed the Sea of Galilee in a boat. When the Savior left the boat, the man ran to Him.

Mark 5:1–2, 6

Jesus told the evil spirit to come out of the man. The evil spirit knew Jesus was the Son of God. He asked Jesus not to hurt him.

Mark 5:7–8

When the Savior asked the evil spirit what his name was, he said, "My name is Legion," which means many. Many evil spirits were in the man. They asked Jesus to let them enter the bodies of some nearby pigs.

Mark 5:9–12

Jesus agreed. The evil spirits left the man and went into the bodies of about 2,000 pigs. The pigs ran down a hill into the sea and drowned.

Mark 5:13

The men who cared for the pigs ran to the city and told people what had happened. The people came and saw Jesus and the wild man. But the man was not wild anymore.

Mark 5:14–15

This made the people afraid of Jesus. They asked Him to go away. He went back to the boat.

Mark 5:15–18

The man who was healed wanted to go with Him. The Savior told him to go home instead and tell his friends what had happened to him.

Mark 5:18–19

The man told his friends, and they were amazed at Jesus's great power.

Mark 5:20

CHAPTER 23

The Man Who Could Not Walk

Ⓞne day Jesus was teaching a group of people in a house.

Luke 5:17

Some men carried their friend on a bed to see Jesus. The friend could not walk. The men could not get him into the house because of all the people.

Luke 5:18–19

The men took their friend up onto the roof. They removed part of the roof and lowered their friend into the house.

Mark 2:4; Luke 5:19

When He saw the great faith of these men, Jesus told the sick man that his sins were forgiven. He told him to pick up his bed and go home. The man stood up. He was healed. He picked up his bed and walked home. He was very thankful to God.

Luke 5:20, 24–25

CHAPTER 24

Jairus's Daughter Is Raised from the Dead

One day Jairus, a ruler of a synagogue, fell at the Savior's feet.

Mark 5:21–22

Jairus said that his 12-year-old daughter was very ill. He begged Jesus to come and bless her. He believed that Jesus could make her better.

Mark 5:23, 42

Jesus started to follow Jairus home, but He stopped to heal a woman. As He was talking to her, someone came to tell Jairus that it was too late—his daughter was dead.

Mark 5:24–35

Jesus heard what was said. He told Jairus not to be afraid but to believe in Him.

Mark 5:36

Then Jesus went with Jairus to Jairus's house. The house was filled with people who were crying because of the little girl's death.

Mark 5:37–38

Jesus told them the girl was not dead but was sleeping. The people laughed at Him. They were sure the girl was dead.

Mark 5:39–40

The Savior had everyone leave the house except
His disciples, Jairus, and Jairus's wife. They went
to the room where the little girl was lying.

Mark 5:40

Jesus took the girl by the hand. He told her to get
up. She stood up and walked. Her parents were
amazed. Jesus told them not to tell anyone what
had happened. Then He told her parents to give
the girl something to eat.

Mark 5:41–43

CHAPTER 25

A Woman Touches Jesus's Clothes

A woman had been very sick for 12 years. She had been to many doctors, but they could not help her.

Mark 5:25–26

One day she saw Jesus surrounded by many people. She believed that she would be healed just by touching His clothing. She walked through the crowd and touched His clothing.

Matthew 9:20–22; Mark 5:27–28

She was healed immediately. Jesus turned around
and asked, "Who touched my clothes?"

Mark 5:29–30

The woman was afraid. She knelt in front of the
Savior and said that she had touched Him. Jesus
told her that her faith in Him had made her well.

Mark 5:33–34

CHAPTER 26

Jesus Forgives
a Woman

APharisee asked the Savior to come to his house and eat with him.

Luke 7:36

A woman who had many sins lived in the city. She knew that Jesus was eating at the Pharisee's house. She wanted to do something special for Jesus.

Luke 7:37

She knelt and washed the Savior's feet with her tears. Then she dried His feet with her hair and kissed them. She put sweet-smelling oil on them too. The Pharisee knew that the woman had done many things that were wrong. He thought that Jesus should not have let the woman touch Him.

Luke 7:38–39

The Savior knew what the Pharisee was thinking. He told the Pharisee that the woman had done more to care for Him than the Pharisee had.

The Pharisee had not given Jesus water to wash His feet or oil for His head, as was often done for guests.

Luke 7:44–46

Jesus told the Pharisee that the woman's sins were forgiven because she loved the Savior and had faith in Him. Jesus told the woman to go in peace.

Luke 7:47–50; Doctrine and Covenants 58:42–43; Jesus the Christ, 262–63

CHAPTER 27

Doing His Father's Work on Earth

On a Jewish feast day, the Savior went to the pool of Bethesda in Jerusalem. People thought that when the water in the pool moved, the first person to step into the water would be healed.

John 5:1–4

Jesus saw a man near the pool who had been unable to walk for 38 years. It was the Sabbath. Jesus asked the man if he wanted to be healed. The man said he could not be healed because he could never get to the water first.

John 5:5–7

Jesus told the man, "Rise, take up thy bed, and walk." The man was immediately healed.

John 5:8–9

Many Jewish people believed that it was a sin
to do miracles on the Sabbath. They wanted to
kill Jesus.

John 5:10–16

Jesus answered that He was doing on the Sabbath
only what His Father would do.

John 5:17

CHAPTER 28

Jesus Feeds 5,000 People

Some friends of John the Baptist told Jesus that John had been killed by the king.

Matthew 14:1–12

When Jesus heard this, He went to a place near the Sea of Galilee to be alone. Many people knew where He was. More than 5,000 people followed Him there hoping that He would teach them.

Matthew 14:13; Mark 6:44

Jesus taught them many things. It was time to eat, but most of the people did not have any food. His disciples wanted Jesus to send the people to the nearest villages to buy food.

Mark 6:34–36

Jesus told the disciples to see if anyone had brought food. They found a boy who had five loaves of bread and two small fish.

Mark 6:37–38; John 6:9

Jesus told all the people to sit down. He blessed the bread and the fish and broke the food into pieces.

Mark 6:39–41

The disciples gave the food to the people. There was more than enough for everyone.

Mark 6:41–44

CHAPTER 29

Jesus Walks on the Water

After feeding the 5,000, Jesus went up on a mountain to pray. His disciples took a boat to cross the Sea of Galilee. When night came, the wind started to blow, and the waves became high.

Matthew 14:22–24

Late that night, Jesus came to join His disciples. He was walking on the water to get to the boat.

Matthew 14:25

The disciples saw Him walking on the water. They were afraid. They thought He was a spirit. Jesus called to them, "It is I; be not afraid."

Matthew 14:26–27

Peter wanted to walk on the water too. Jesus told Peter to come to Him. Peter climbed out of the boat. He began to walk on the water toward the Savior.

Matthew 14:28–29

Because the wind was blowing hard, Peter became afraid. He began to sink into the water and cried out to Jesus to save him.

Matthew 14:30

The Savior took Peter's hand. He asked Peter why he did not have more faith.

Matthew 14:31

When Jesus and Peter came to the boat, the storm stopped. All the disciples worshipped the Savior. They knew that He was the Son of God.

Matthew 14:32–33

CHAPTER 30

The Bread of Life

The next day many people tried to find Jesus. They followed Him to Capernaum in boats.

John 6:22, 24

Jesus knew that they wanted Him to feed them again.

John 6:26

Jesus taught them that bread could keep them alive for only a short time. He said that there was another kind of bread they should look for—the Bread of Life. He told them that He was the Bread of Life.

John 6:27, 32–35

Jesus taught the people that He would sacrifice His life for them. He said that if they would follow and believe in Him, they would gain everlasting life.

John 6:47–51

CHAPTER 31

Jesus Heals a Deaf Man

Some people brought a man to Jesus. The man was deaf and could not talk well. The people wanted the Savior to heal him.

Mark 7:32

Jesus led the man away from the others. He put His fingers in the man's ears. He touched the man's tongue and blessed him.

Mark 7:33–34

Now the man could hear and talk. The people could understand him. Jesus asked the people not to tell anyone what had happened, but they told everyone.

Mark 7:35–36

CHAPTER 32

Peter Testifies of Christ

Jesus asked His disciples who the people thought He was.

Matthew 16:13; Mark 8:27; Luke 9:18

The disciples answered that some people thought Jesus was John the Baptist. Others thought He was an Old Testament prophet who had come back from the dead.

Matthew 16:14; Mark 8:28; Luke 9:19

Jesus asked His disciples who they thought He was. Peter said, "Thou art the Christ, the Son of the living God."

Matthew 16:15–16; Mark 8:29; Luke 9:20

Jesus explained that Peter's testimony had not come from the learning of men. His testimony had come by revelation from God.

Matthew 16:17

Jesus promised Peter that He would give him the priesthood and the authority to lead His Church. Then Peter and the disciples would have the authority to set up Jesus's Church on earth.

Matthew 16:18–19

Jesus told His disciples not to tell anyone yet that He was the Christ. First He needed to suffer, be killed, and rise from the dead on the third day.

Matthew 16:20; Mark 8:30–31; Luke 9:21–22

77

CHAPTER 33

Appearing in Glory: The Transfiguration

Jesus took Peter, James, and John to the top of a high mountain to pray.

Matthew 17:1; Mark 9:2; Luke 9:28

As Jesus prayed, the glory of God came upon Him. His face was bright like the sun. Two Old Testament prophets named Moses and Elias appeared to Him. They talked about His coming death and resurrection.

Matthew 17:2–3; Mark 9:3–4; Luke 9:29–31 (see footnote 31a)

While Jesus was praying, the Apostles fell asleep.

Luke 9:32

When they awoke, they saw the glory of Jesus Christ, Moses, and Elias. They heard Heavenly Father's voice testify, "This is my beloved Son, in whom I am well pleased; hear ye him."

Matthew 17:5; Mark 9:7; Luke 9:32, 35

The Apostles were afraid and fell to the ground. Jesus touched them and told them not to fear. When they looked up, the heavenly messengers were gone. Jesus told the Apostles not to tell anyone what they had seen until after He had died and been resurrected.

Matthew 17:6–9; Mark 9:8–9

CHAPTER 34

The Boy with an Evil Spirit

One day a man asked the Savior to help his son. The boy had an evil spirit in him. The disciples had already tried to heal his son, but they could not.

Mark 9:14–18

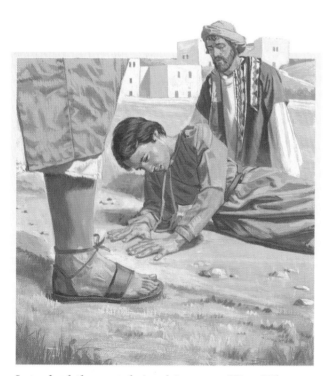

Jesus had the man bring his son to Him. When the boy came, the evil spirit made him fall to the ground.

Mark 9:19–20

The Savior asked how long the evil spirit had been in the boy. The father said that it had been in him since he was a child.

Mark 9:21

Jesus said that He could heal the son if the father had faith. The father began to cry. He said that he had faith. But he asked Jesus to help him have even more faith.

Mark 9:23–24

Jesus commanded the evil spirit to come out of the boy and never go into him again. The evil spirit was angry. It hurt the boy again. Then it obeyed Jesus and left.

Mark 9:25–26

The boy was so quiet that many people said he was dead. But Jesus took his hand and helped him stand up. The boy was healed. The evil spirit was gone.

Mark 9:26–27

Later the disciples asked Jesus why they had not been able to make the evil spirit leave the boy. Jesus told them that sometimes they needed to fast and pray in order for a person to be healed.

Matthew 17:20–21; Mark 9:28–29

81

CHAPTER 35

The Good Samaritan

Jesus told many stories, or parables, to help people learn the truth.

One day a leader of the Jews asked Jesus what he must do to have eternal life. The Savior asked him what the scriptures said. The leader said that a man should love God and also love his neighbor. Jesus said that he was right. Then the leader asked, "Who is my neighbour?"

Luke 10:25–29

Jesus answered by telling the man a story. One day a Jewish man was walking on the road to the city of Jericho. Thieves robbed and beat him. They left the man on the road, almost dead.

Luke 10:30

Soon a Jewish priest came by and saw the man. The priest walked by on the other side of the road. He did not help the man.

Luke 10:31

Another Jewish man who worked in the temple came by. He saw the injured man. But he did not help the man either and walked by on the other side of the road.

Luke 10:32

Then a Samaritan man came along. The Jews and the Samaritans did not get along. But when the Samaritan saw the man, he felt sorry for him.

He took care of the man's wounds and put clothes on him.

Luke 10:33–34; John 4:9;
Bible Dictionary, "Samaritans," 768

83

The Samaritan took the man to an inn and cared for him until the next day. When the Samaritan had to leave, he gave money to the innkeeper and told him to take care of the man.

Luke 10:34–35

After Jesus told this story, He asked the Jewish leader which of the three men was a neighbor to the injured man.

Luke 10:36

The leader said that the Samaritan was because he had helped the man. Jesus told the Jewish leader to be like the Samaritan.

Luke 10:37

CHAPTER 36

Jesus Tells Three Parables

One day Jesus was eating and talking with people who many thought were sinners. Some Pharisees saw Him.

Luke 15:1–2

The Pharisees believed that good men should not talk to sinners. They thought that Jesus was not a good man because he was talking to sinners.

Luke 15:2

The Savior wanted to help the Pharisees understand why He was with the sinners. He told them three parables. The first one was about a lost sheep.

Luke 15:3; Teachings of the Prophet Joseph Smith, 277

The Lost Sheep

A good shepherd had 100 sheep. One of them was lost.

Luke 15:4

The shepherd left the 99 sheep to look for the lost one. When he found it, he was very happy.

Luke 15:4–5

The shepherd carried the sheep home. He called to all his friends and neighbors to come and be happy with him. He had found the lost sheep.

Luke 15:5–6

Jesus Christ told the Pharisees what the parable meant. He said that those who sin are like the lost sheep.

Luke 15:7

Just as the shepherd wanted to save the lost sheep, Jesus wants to save those who sin.

Mark 2:17

Jesus said that was why He was talking with sinners.

Matthew 18:11 (see footnote 11c); Mark 2:17

And just as the shepherd was very happy when he found the lost sheep, Jesus is very happy when we repent.

Luke 15:6–7

The Lost Coin

A woman had 10 silver coins. She lost one of the coins. She looked all over the house for it.

Luke 15:8

At last she found the coin. She was very happy. She called her friends and neighbors to tell them.

They too were happy that she had found the lost coin.

Luke 15:9

Church leaders and members are like the woman in the story; the lost coin is like a member of the Church who does not go to church or try to live the commandments anymore. It is as if they are lost from the Church. Jesus Christ wants Church members to find any lost brothers or sisters and help them come back to Him. He is very happy when this happens.

Jesus the Christ, 455–56

The friends and neighbors in the story are like the angels of God. The angels are very happy when a person repents.

Luke 15:10

The Lost Son

A man had two sons. The man promised to give his money to them when he died. The younger son did not want to wait. He asked his father for his part of the money. His father gave it to him.

Luke 15:11–12

The son took the money and left home. He went to another land. The son sinned again and again. He spent all of the money.

Luke 15:13

Finally the son had no money to buy food. He was very hungry. He asked a man for help. The man hired him to feed his pigs.

Luke 15:14–15

The son was so hungry that he wanted to eat the pigs' food. He knew that the servants in his father's house had better food to eat than he did.

Luke 15:16–17

He decided to repent and ask to be a servant in his father's house. When the son went home, his father saw him coming.

Luke 15:18–20

The father ran to meet his son. He put his arms around him and kissed him.

Luke 15:20

The son told his father that he had sinned. He felt
he was not worthy to be called his father's son.

Luke 15:21

The father told a servant to bring the best clothes and put them on the son. The servant put shoes on the son's feet and a ring on his finger.

Luke 15:22

The father told the servant to prepare a feast. He wanted everyone to celebrate. The son who had sinned had repented and returned home.

Luke 15:23–24

The older son had been working in the field. When he came home, he heard music and dancing. A servant told him that his younger brother had come home. His father wanted everyone to celebrate.

Luke 15:25–27

The older son was angry and would not go into the house. His father came out to talk with him.

Luke 15:28

The father was thankful that the older son had always stayed with him. Everything the father had would be his. The father also said that it was right to celebrate. He was happy his younger son had repented and returned home.

Luke 15:31–32

Jesus told the Pharisees the three parables because He wanted them to know how much Heavenly Father loves everyone. He loves people who obey Him. He also loves sinners, but Heavenly Father cannot bless them until they repent. He wants sinners to repent and come back to Him. And He wants us to help them do that and to be happy when they return.

John 3:16–17

The Ten Lepers

Jesus went to a small town where He saw ten lepers. Lepers are people who are sick. Their sickness causes them to get terrible sores all over their bodies.

Luke 17:12

Doctors could not help the lepers. People were afraid to go near them. They did not want to get sick too.

Luke 17:12

The lepers asked Jesus to heal them. They knew He could make their sores go away.

Luke 17:13

Jesus wanted them to be well. He told them to go and show themselves to the priests.

Luke 17:14

On their way to the priests, the ten lepers were healed. Their sores were gone.

Luke 17:14

One of the lepers knew that Jesus had healed them. He went back to thank Him. Jesus asked where the other nine lepers were. They had not come back. Jesus told the leper who had thanked Him that the leper's faith had made him well.

Luke 17:15–19

The Pharisee and the Publican

One day the Savior talked to some people who thought that they were more righteous than other people. Jesus told them a story.

Luke 18:9

Two men went to the temple to pray. One was a Pharisee. The other was a publican, which is a tax collector. People did not like tax collectors. They thought tax collectors were not honest.

Luke 18:10

The Pharisee stood in front of others to pray. He thanked God that he was better than other people. He said that he fasted two times each week and paid his tithing. The publican stood by himself, bowed his head, and prayed, "God be merciful to me a sinner."

Luke 18:11–13

The Pharisee thought he was perfect and did not need God's help. But the publican knew that he was not perfect and needed God's help. He was humble and asked God to forgive him.

Luke 18:14

Jesus said that people should be like the publican. They should not think they are better than other people. They should repent of their sins and ask God to forgive them.

Luke 18:14

CHAPTER 39

Jesus Heals a Blind Man

One day Jesus was walking with His disciples. They saw a man who had been born blind. The disciples asked if the man was blind because he had sinned or because his parents had sinned.

John 9:1–2

The Savior said that neither the parents nor the man had sinned. The man was blind so that Jesus could heal him and show people God's power.

John 9:3–5

Jesus made clay out of the dirt. He put it on the blind man's eyes. Jesus told the man to go wash his eyes.

John 9:6–7

As soon as the man washed the clay from his eyes, he could see!

John 9:7

When his neighbors saw him, they were not sure who he was. He told them that Jesus had healed him. The neighbors took the man to the Pharisees. The man told the Pharisees that Jesus had healed him.

John 9:8–11

Some of the Pharisees thought Jesus must be a righteous man. Others thought He was a sinner. When the man said Jesus was a righteous person, some of the Pharisees were angry and threw the man out.

John 9:13–16, 30–34

Jesus found the man. He asked the man if he believed in the Son of God. The man asked who the Son of God was. Jesus said that He was the Son of God, and the man worshipped Him.

John 9:35–38

CHAPTER 40

The Good Shepherd

A shepherd takes care of sheep. He helps them find food and water. He does not let them get hurt or lost. He knows them and loves them and would give his life to save them.

John 10:11–15

Jesus Christ called Himself the Good Shepherd. He is our shepherd. We are His sheep. He loves us. He helps us learn the truth. He teaches us how to live so we can return to Heavenly Father. He gave His life for us.

John 10:11–15

The Savior told the people in Jerusalem that He had other sheep. He said He would visit these other sheep. The people did not understand.

John 10:16; 3 Nephi 15:21–22, 24

After Jesus was resurrected, He visited His sheep in the Americas. The Book of Mormon tells about His visit there. Jesus stayed many days, healing the sick and blessing the people. He gave them the priesthood and organized His Church. Jesus taught the same things to these people that He had taught to the people in Jerusalem.

3 Nephi 11–28

Jesus Blesses the Children

Jesus was going to Jerusalem. Along the way some people wanted Jesus to bless their children. The disciples told the people not to bother Jesus.

Mark 10:13

But Jesus Christ loves children. He told the disciples to let the children come to Him. Jesus also told the disciples that they should be like little children. Then they could live with God in heaven.

Mark 10:14–15

104

CHAPTER 42

The Rich Young Man

One day a rich young man came to Jesus and asked Him what he should do to go to heaven.

Mark 10:17

The Savior told him to love and honor his father and mother and not to kill anyone or lie or steal. The rich young man said he had always obeyed the commandments.

Mark 10:19–20

Jesus told the young man that he needed to do one more thing. He needed to sell everything he had and give the money to the poor. Then the young man should follow Him.

Mark 10:21

The rich young man did not want to give away everything he had. He loved the things he owned more than he loved God. The young man left feeling sad.

Mark 10:22

The Savior told His disciples that it is hard for those who love riches to go to heaven. The disciples did not understand. They asked who can live with God. Jesus said that people who trust God and love Him more than anything else can live with Him in heaven.

Mark 10:23–30 (see footnote 27a)

CHAPTER 43

Jesus Brings Lazarus Back to Life

A man named Lazarus lived in Bethany with his sisters Mary and Martha. Jesus loved Lazarus and his sisters, and they loved Jesus.

John 11:1–2, 5

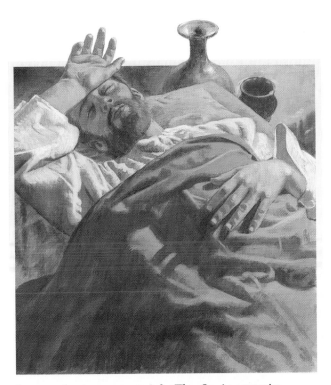

Lazarus became very sick. The Savior was in another town. Mary and Martha sent word to Him that Lazarus was sick.

John 11:3

The Savior asked His disciples to go with Him to help Lazarus. The disciples were afraid to go to Bethany. It was near Jerusalem. Some people in Jerusalem wanted to kill Jesus.

John 11:6–8, 18

Jesus told His disciples that Lazarus was dead. He said that He would bring him back to life. This miracle would help the disciples know that He was the Savior. Jesus went to Bethany. When He got there, Lazarus had been dead for four days.

John 11:11–17, 19

Martha told Jesus that Lazarus would still be alive if He had come sooner. Jesus said Lazarus would live again. He asked Martha if she believed Him. Martha said yes. She knew that Jesus was the Savior.

John 11:20–27

Martha left Jesus to get her sister, Mary. Mary went to meet Jesus too. Many people followed her. Mary knelt, crying, at the Savior's feet.

The people with her were also crying. Jesus asked where Lazarus's body was.

John 11:28–34

Jesus went to the cave where Lazarus was buried. There was a stone in front of it. He told the people to move the stone.

John 11:38–39

Jesus looked up. He thanked Heavenly Father for hearing His prayers.

John 11:41–42

Then, in a loud voice, Jesus told Lazarus to come out of the cave. Lazarus walked out. Many of the people who saw the miracle now believed that Jesus was the Savior.

John 11:43–45

CHAPTER 44

The Savior Goes to Jerusalem

Some people told the priests and the Pharisees that Jesus had brought Lazarus back to life. The Pharisees thought that everyone would believe in Jesus. They were afraid that no one would listen to them.

John 11:46–48

The Pharisees planned a way to kill Jesus. They waited for Him to come to Jerusalem for the Passover feast.

John 11:49–51, 55–57

Jesus went to Jerusalem. Many people heard that He was coming and went to meet Him. Jesus rode a young donkey into the city. A prophet had written that the Son of God would do this. Many people believed that Jesus was the Son of God. They put palm branches and some of their clothes on the ground for Him to ride over. They shouted hosanna and said that Jesus was their king.

Zechariah 9:9; Matthew 21:4–9; John 12:1, 12–15

People in Jerusalem came to see what was happening. They asked who Jesus was. People in the crowd told them that He was a prophet from Nazareth.

Matthew 21:10–11

The Pharisees were angry. They did not want people to believe that Jesus was the Savior. Jesus knew the Pharisees wanted to kill Him.

John 11:53; 12:19, 23

Jesus told His disciples that He would soon die. He would suffer for the sins of all people and then die on a cross. He was the Savior of the world. This was why He had come to earth.

John 12:23–25, 27, 32–33, 47

The Widow's Mites

Jesus went to the temple in Jerusalem. He watched as people gave money for the church. Many rich people gave a lot of money.

Mark 12:41

A poor widow gave two pieces of money called mites. It was not very much money, but it was all the money she had.

Mark 12:42, 44

Jesus saw the widow and told the disciples what she had done.

Mark 12:43

He said the rich people had given a greater amount of money than she had, but they had more to give.

Mark 12:43–44

The widow had no more money. She gave all that she had. She gave more to God than all the rich people.

Mark 12:44

CHAPTER 46

The Second Coming

Jesus was on the Mount of Olives. His disciples wanted to ask Jesus some questions. They asked when the wicked would be destroyed. They also wanted to know when Jesus would come again.

Matthew 24:3; Joseph Smith—Matthew 1:4

Jesus told them that before His Second Coming, false prophets would claim to be the Christ. Many people would follow them. But if His followers obeyed His words, they would not be fooled by the false prophets. They would be saved.

Matthew 24:4–5, 24–27; Mark 13:21–22; Joseph Smith—Matthew 1:21–22, 37

Jesus also said that before He comes again, there will be many wars, famines, terrible sicknesses, and earthquakes. Many people will stop helping others and become wicked.

Doctrine and Covenants 45:16, 26–27, 31–32;
Joseph Smith—Matthew 1:23, 28–30

The gospel will be preached to the whole world, but many people will not listen.

Doctrine and Covenants 45:28–29; Joseph Smith—Matthew 1:31

The sun will be darkened, the moon will not shine, and stars will fall from heaven.

Matthew 24:29; Mark 13:24–25; Joseph Smith—Matthew 1:33

When Jesus Christ comes again, people will see Him coming down from the clouds with power and great glory. He will send His angels to gather the righteous together.

Matthew 24:30–31; Mark 13:26–27; Joseph Smith—Matthew 1:36–37

We can prepare for the Second Coming by doing what is right. When we see the signs Jesus promised, we will know that the Savior's coming is near. No one knows exactly when Jesus will come again. If we are prepared, we can be with Him.

Matthew 24:44; Luke 21:36; Joseph Smith—Matthew 1:39–40

CHAPTER 47

The Ten Virgins

Jesus told a story about ten young women who went to a wedding. They waited for the bridegroom to come and let them in. They did not know what time he would come.

Matthew 25:1, 13

The ten women had oil-burning lamps. Five of the women were wise. They had extra oil with them.

Matthew 25:2, 4

The other five women were foolish. They only had the oil that was in their lamps.

Matthew 25:3

The bridegroom did not come for a long time. The oil in the lamps ran out. The five wise women had more oil to put in their lamps. The five foolish women had to go buy more oil.

Matthew 25:5–9

While they were gone, the bridegroom came. He let the five wise women into the wedding.

Matthew 25:10

When the five foolish women returned, the door was closed. They could not go to the wedding.

Matthew 25:10–12

Jesus is like the bridegroom in this story. Church members are like the ten women. When Jesus comes again, some members will be ready. They will have obeyed God's commandments. Others will not be ready. They will not be able to be with the Savior when He comes again.

Matthew 25:13; Doctrine and Covenants 45:56–57; 88:86, 92;
Jesus the Christ, *576–80*

CHAPTER 48

The Talents

Jesus told His disciples a story about a man who gave his servants some talents. A talent was a large amount of money.

Matthew 25:14–15

The man gave one servant five talents. He gave another servant two talents. He gave a third servant one talent. Then the man went on a journey.

Matthew 25:15

The servant with five talents worked hard. He earned five more talents. He now had ten talents.

Matthew 25:16

121

The servant with two talents also worked hard. He earned two more talents. He now had four talents.

Matthew 25:17

The servant with one talent buried it in the ground. He was afraid he would lose it. He did not work to earn any more talents.

Matthew 25:18

When the man came back, he asked the servants what they had done with his talents.

Matthew 25:19

The first servant brought him ten talents. The man was happy. He made the servant a leader over many things and told him to be joyful.

Matthew 25:20–21

The second servant brought the man four talents. This also made the man happy. He made the second servant a leader over many things and told him to be joyful.

Matthew 25:22–23

The third servant gave the man back the talent he had buried. The man was not happy. He said the servant was lazy. He should have worked hard to earn more talents.

Matthew 25:24–27

The man took the talent from the third servant and gave it to the first servant. Then he sent the lazy servant away. The man in the story is like Jesus. We are like the servants. Jesus will judge how we each use the gifts we have been given.

Matthew 25:28–30

CHAPTER 49

The First Sacrament

Every year the Jews held a feast called the Passover. It helped the Jewish people remember that God had saved their ancestors at the time of Moses.

Exodus 12:27; Luke 22:7

Jesus and the Twelve Apostles needed a place to eat the Passover feast. The Savior sent Peter and

John to find a room and see that everything was ready for the feast.

Luke 22:8

They found a room and prepared the feast.

Luke 22:9–13

Jesus and all the Apostles went there. They ate the Passover feast together.

Luke 22:14

Jesus gave His Apostles the sacrament for the first time. He took bread in His hands, blessed it, and then broke it into pieces. He told the Apostles to eat the bread.

Matthew 26:26; Luke 22:19

Jesus told them to think of His body when they ate the bread. He asked them to remember that He would die for them.

Matthew 26:26; Luke 22:19

Jesus poured wine into a cup. He blessed the wine and told the Apostles to drink it.

Matthew 26:27

Jesus told them to think of His blood when they drank the wine. He asked them to remember that He would bleed and suffer for the sins of all people.

Matthew 26:28; Luke 22:20

Jesus also told the Apostles that wicked men would soon kill Him. Eleven of the Apostles were very sad. They loved the Savior and did not want Him to die. Jesus knew that one of the Apostles would help the wicked men. His name was Judas Iscariot.

Matthew 26:2, 14–16, 21–25

CHAPTER 50

Other Teachings at the Last Supper

After they finished eating, Jesus told His Apostles that they should love one another as He had loved them. If they did this, people would know they were His disciples.

John 13:34–35

He said that if the Apostles loved Him, they would keep His commandments. He promised them the gift of the Holy Ghost. The Holy Ghost would teach them all they needed to know. The Holy Ghost would help the Apostles remember the things Jesus had taught them.

John 14:15–18, 26

Jesus said that He was like a vine. His disciples are like branches of the vine. Only a branch that is firmly attached to the vine can produce good fruit.

John 15:1–2, 5

Jesus promised His Apostles that if they lived the gospel, their fruit (their works) would be good. If they did not follow Him, they would be like branches cut off from a plant and produce nothing.

John 15:3–8

Jesus Christ prayed that His Apostles would be united. He wanted them to teach people to believe in Him and to know that Heavenly Father loves them.

John 17:1–4, 6, 11, 20–23

Then Jesus and the Apostles sang a hymn and left the room.

Matthew 26:30

CHAPTER 51

Jesus Suffers in the Garden of Gethsemane

Jesus and the Apostles went to the Garden of Gethsemane. Judas did not go with them. He went to tell the Jewish leaders where Jesus was.

Matthew 26:36; Mark 14:43; John 18:2–3

The Savior asked Peter, James, and John to go with Him into the garden. He asked them to wait while He went to pray.

Matthew 26:36–39; Mark 14:33–35

Jesus knew He needed to suffer for the sins of all
people. He did not want to suffer, but He chose
to obey Heavenly Father.

Matthew 26:39–44

Peter, James, and John fell asleep while Jesus
prayed. Jesus came and found them sleeping.
He asked them to stay awake.

Matthew 26:40–41

He went to pray again. Peter, James, and John
wanted to stay awake, but they were very tired.

They fell asleep again. Jesus again found them
sleeping. He went and prayed a third time.

Matthew 26:42–44

As Jesus prayed, He began to tremble because of the pain. An angel came to strengthen Him. He suffered so much that he sweat drops of blood.

He was suffering for all of our sins so that we can be forgiven if we repent.

Luke 22:41–44; Doctrine and Covenants 19:16–19

Jesus woke Peter, James, and John. He told them that He would be betrayed and killed. Jesus said that wicked people were coming to take Him away.

Matthew 26:45–46

CHAPTER 52

The Trials of Jesus

The leaders of the Jews sent men with swords and sticks to the Garden of Gethsemane.

Matthew 26:47

Judas Iscariot was with them. The chief priests had paid Judas to show the men where Jesus was.

Matthew 26:14–16, 47

Judas showed the men who Jesus was by kissing Him. The men led Jesus away. They mocked and hit Him. Then they took Jesus to the high priest, Caiaphas.

Matthew 26:48–49, 57; Luke 22:54, 63–65

The Jewish leaders asked Jesus questions. They said that He had broken the law by saying that He was the Son of God. Jesus told them that He was the Son of God. They said Jesus was guilty and should die.

Luke 22:66–71

The Jewish leaders did not have the authority to kill Jesus. They took Him to Pontius Pilate, who could sentence Jesus to die. The Jewish leaders told Pilate that Jesus had taught the people to disobey the Roman law.

Luke 23:1–2

Pilate did not think Jesus had done anything wrong. Pilate wanted to let Jesus go. The crowd wanted Jesus to be crucified.

Luke 23:14–21

Pilate still wanted to let Jesus go. But the priests
and the people kept shouting that they wanted
Jesus to be crucified.

Luke 23:22–23

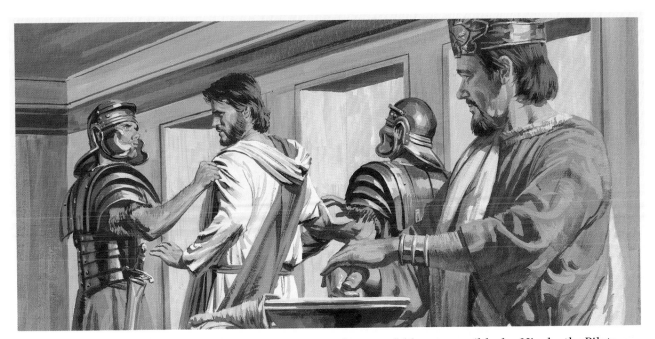

Pilate washed his hands. He said that he was not
responsible for Jesus's death. The people said that
they would be responsible for His death. Pilate
told his soldiers to crucify Jesus.

Matthew 27:24–26

CHAPTER 53

Jesus Is Crucified

The soldiers beat Jesus with whips. They put a purple robe on Him. They made a crown of thorns and put it on Jesus's head. They laughed at Him and spit on Him. They called Him "King of the Jews."

Mark 15:15–20

Many people followed the soldiers as they took Jesus to a hill near Jerusalem. They made Him carry His own cross. They nailed His hands and feet to the cross and lifted it up. They also crucified two other men, who were thieves.

Luke 23:27, 33; John 19:17–18

Jesus prayed. He asked Heavenly Father to forgive
the soldiers who crucified Him. They did not
know that He was the Savior.

Luke 23:34

Mary, the mother of Jesus, was standing by the
cross. The Apostle John was there too. Jesus told
John to take care of His mother. John took Jesus's
mother to his home.

John 19:25–27

Darkness covered the land. The Savior suffered on the cross for many hours. Finally His spirit left His body, and He died.

Matthew 27:45, 50

When He died, an earthquake broke huge rocks into pieces. A curtain in the temple, called the veil, was torn in two. The Roman soldiers were afraid.

Matthew 27:51, 54

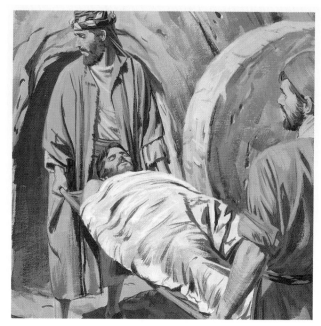

One of Jesus's disciples took the Savior's body off the cross. He wrapped it in a cloth and placed it in a tomb, a place where people are buried. A big rock was rolled in front of the tomb.

Matthew 27:57–60

CHAPTER 54

Jesus Is Risen

The Savior's body was in the tomb until Sunday morning. Then two angels came and rolled the stone away from the tomb.

Matthew 28:1–2 (see footnote 2a); Luke 24:1–4

A woman whom Jesus had healed named Mary Magdalene went to the tomb. She was surprised to see that the stone had been moved. Jesus's body was not in the tomb.

John 20:1–2

She ran to tell Peter and John that someone had taken the Savior's body. She did not know where it was.

John 20:2

Peter and John ran to the tomb. They found the cloth Jesus had been buried in, but Jesus's body was not there. Peter and John did not know what to do. They went home.

John 20:3–7, 10

Mary Magdalene stayed by the tomb, crying. When she looked into the tomb again, she saw two angels.

John 20:11–12

They asked Mary Magdalene why she was crying. She said someone had taken Jesus's body away. She did not know where it was.

John 20:13

She turned around and saw someone. She thought it was the gardener. He asked her why she was crying. She asked Him if He knew where Jesus's body was.

John 20:14–15

Then the man said, "Mary," and she knew it was Jesus. He asked her to tell the Apostles that He was resurrected.

John 20:15–17

Mary Magdalene and some other women told the
Apostles that Jesus had been resurrected. At first
the Apostles did not believe them.

Luke 24:10–11; John 20:18

Later, while the Apostles were talking to each
other, Jesus came into the room. The Apostles
were afraid. They still thought He was dead.

Luke 24:36–37

The Savior told them to touch His hands and feet.
He was resurrected—His body and spirit had come
together again.

Luke 24:38–40

143

The Apostles were happy to see Him. He
asked them for food. They gave Him fish
and honeycomb. He ate it.

Luke 24:41–43

Jesus Christ was the first person to be resurrected.
Many others were then resurrected and seen by
people living in Jerusalem. Jesus had said, "I am
the resurrection, and the life." Because He over-
came death, we will all be resurrected someday.

Matthew 27:52–53; John 11:25

CHAPTER 55

The Apostles Lead the Church

After He was resurrected, Jesus stayed with His Apostles for 40 days. He taught them many things about the gospel and His Church.

Acts 1:1–3

He told them to teach the gospel to all people. He also said that He would leave them soon, but the Holy Ghost would come to help them.

Acts 1:4–8

The Apostles watched Jesus go up into the clouds.
Two angels in white clothes told the Apostles that
Jesus would come back from heaven someday.

Acts 1:9–11

146

The Apostles were now the leaders of the Church of Jesus Christ on earth. Peter was President, and James and John were his counselors.

Matthew 16:18–19; Doctrine and Covenants 81:1–2; Jesus the Christ, 219–20

There were only eleven Apostles—Judas was dead. Heavenly Father told the Apostles to choose Matthias to be one of the Twelve Apostles. All of the Apostles had a special calling in the priesthood.

Matthew 27:3–5; Acts 1:15–17, 21–26; Doctrine and Covenants 102:8

The Apostles and the other disciples had faith in the Lord. They obeyed His commandments. They loved one another.

Acts 2:41–47

With the priesthood and the power of the Holy Ghost, the Apostles could do many things. They healed the sick and were missionaries. They taught about Jesus Christ and His gospel. Many people believed the Apostles' words and joined the Church. Church members were called Saints.

Acts 2:2–4, 32–33, 36–43, 47; 3:1–8; Romans 1:7

147

CHAPTER 56

Peter Heals a Man

A man who could not walk was carried to the temple every day. He sat by the temple doors and asked for money. One day he saw Peter and John about to enter the temple.

Acts 3:1–3

He asked Peter and John for money. Peter said that he did not have any money. Peter said that he would give the man something else.

Acts 3:3, 6

Peter blessed the man in the name of Jesus Christ and healed him. Then he helped the man stand up.

Acts 3:6–7

The man walked for the first time in his life. Many people saw the man walking and leaping. They knew it was a miracle. They knew Peter had the power of God. Peter told them that Jesus Christ had given him the power to heal the man. Peter was a great missionary. He helped many people believe in and follow Jesus Christ.

Acts 3:8–13, 16; 4:4

CHAPTER 57

Wicked Men Kill Stephen

Many Jewish leaders thought that miracles would stop when Jesus died. However, the Apostles also performed miracles. Many people believed in Jesus Christ and joined the Church.

Acts 4:1–4, 13–16; 5:14

This made many Jewish leaders angry. They put Peter and John in prison. King Herod Agrippa had the Apostle James killed.

Acts 4:3; 12:1–2

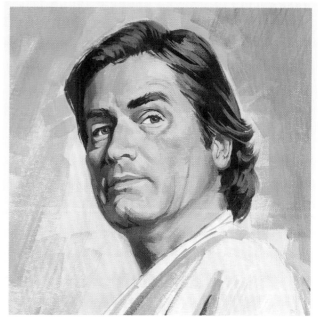

The Apostles called seven men to help lead the Church. One was a righteous man named Stephen. He taught the gospel to many people. Some wicked people lied and said that Stephen spoke against Jewish law. They took him to be tried by the Jewish leaders.

Acts 6:3–12

Stephen told the leaders that they were wicked. He said that they had killed Jesus Christ, the Son of God.

Acts 7:51–54

Then Stephen looked up into heaven and saw Heavenly Father and Jesus Christ. When he told the leaders what he saw, they were very angry.

Acts 7:55–56

They took Stephen out of the city to kill him by throwing stones at him. They laid their coats at the feet of a young man named Saul. As Stephen was dying, he asked God to take his spirit to heaven. He also asked God to forgive those who were killing him. Then he died.

Acts 7:58–60

Simon and
the Priesthood

Many people in Samaria heard and believed the gospel. They were baptized, but they did not have the Holy Ghost.

Acts 8:5, 12–16

Peter and John went to Samaria. They laid their hands on people's heads and gave them the gift of the Holy Ghost.

Acts 8:14–17

A man named Simon saw Peter and John giving people the gift of the Holy Ghost. Simon knew that the two Apostles could give people the gift of the Holy Ghost because they had the priesthood. He wanted the priesthood too.

Acts 8:9, 18–19

He offered Peter and John money for it. Peter told Simon that no one can buy the priesthood. God gives it to righteous men. Peter knew that Simon was not righteous. He told him to repent.

Acts 8:18–24

CHAPTER 59

Saul Learns about Jesus

Saul had watched the people kill Stephen. One day Saul was walking to the city of Damascus with some friends. He wanted to put some of Christ's disciples in prison.

Acts 7:58; 9:1–2

Suddenly a bright light from heaven surrounded him. He fell to the ground. Then Saul heard the voice of Jesus asking him why he was trying to hurt the Saints. Saul was afraid. He asked Jesus what he should do. The Savior said Saul should go to Damascus. There Saul would be told what he needed to do.

Acts 9:3–6

Saul opened his eyes, but he could not see. He was blind. His friends took him to Damascus.

Acts 9:8–9

A disciple of Jesus Christ named Ananias lived in Damascus. In a vision, Jesus told Ananias to go to Saul.

Acts 9:10–11

Ananias had the priesthood. He put his hands on Saul's head and blessed him that Saul's sight would come back. After being healed, Saul was baptized and received the gift of the Holy Ghost.

Acts 9:17–18

Saul changed his name to Paul. He was called to be an Apostle. He became a missionary for the Church. He wrote many letters. He went to many lands and taught the gospel.

Acts 26:16–23; Romans 1:1

CHAPTER 60

Peter Brings Tabitha Back to Life

A good woman named Tabitha lived in the city of Joppa. She was a follower of Jesus Christ. She helped many people and did many good things.

Acts 9:36

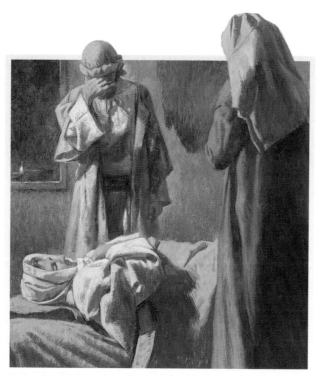

She became sick and died.

Acts 9:37

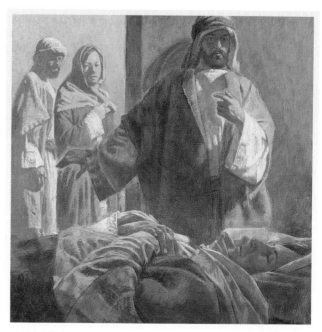

Her friends sent for Peter. When he got there, he asked Tabitha's friends to leave the room.

Acts 9:38–40

Peter knelt and prayed, then told Tabitha to
stand. She opened her eyes and sat up.

Acts 9:40

Peter helped her stand. He called her friends.
They came and saw that she was alive. Peter had
used the power of the priesthood to bring Tabitha
back to life. Many people in Joppa believed
in Jesus Christ when they learned of Tabitha's
return to life.

Acts 9:41–42

CHAPTER 61

Paul and Silas in Prison

A girl had an evil spirit in her. People liked to hear what the evil spirit said through her. They paid the men she worked for to hear the evil spirit speak.

Acts 16:16

Whenever Paul and Silas walked by, the girl followed them. As she did, the evil spirit spoke. One day Paul commanded the evil spirit to leave her. It did. The men she worked for were angry. Now they could not make money.

Acts 16:17–19

The men took Paul and Silas to the leaders of their city. They said that Paul and Silas had been causing trouble.

Acts 16:19–22

The leaders had Paul and Silas whipped and put in prison.

Acts 16:22–24

That night Paul and Silas prayed and sang hymns to Heavenly Father. Everyone in the prison heard them. Suddenly the ground began to shake. The prison doors opened.

Acts 16:25–26

The guard woke up and saw the open doors. He thought the prisoners had escaped. Paul told the guard not to worry. The prisoners were all still there. The guard knelt by Paul and Silas and asked how he could be saved.

Acts 16:27–30

Paul and Silas taught the guard and his family the gospel. That night the guard and his family were baptized.

Acts 16:31–33

The next day the city leaders set Paul and Silas free. Paul and Silas went to another city to do more missionary work.

Acts 16:35–40

CHAPTER 62

Paul Obeys the Holy Ghost

The Holy Ghost told the Apostle Paul to go to Jerusalem. The Holy Ghost said that Paul would be put in prison. Paul was not afraid. He loved the Savior and did what the Holy Ghost had told him to do.

Acts 20:22–24

Paul said good-bye to his friends. He said he would never see them again. He told them to live the gospel and obey God's commandments. Paul warned them not to listen to people who would try to teach them things that are not true.

Acts 20:25, 28–32

Paul told them to love and take care of each other. He knelt and prayed with them. Everyone cried. They went with him to the boat and watched Paul leave for Jerusalem.

Acts 20:35–38

161

CHAPTER 63

Paul Finishes His Mission

Paul went to the temple in Jerusalem. A group of Jews thought Paul had taken people who were not Jews into the temple. This made the Jewish people angry. They took Paul out of the temple and beat him.

Acts 21:26–32

Roman soldiers arrested Paul. They let him speak to the Jewish people. Paul testified to the people that he had seen a light from heaven and heard the Savior's voice. He said that Jesus had told him to preach the gospel.

Acts 21:33–40; 22:1–15

The people did not believe Paul. They wanted to kill him. The soldiers put Paul in prison for the night.

Acts 22:22–30

The Savior visited Paul in prison and told him not
to be afraid. He said Paul would go to Rome and
teach the gospel there.

Acts 23:11

To protect Paul, the Romans sent him to another city. King Agrippa was there. Paul told King Agrippa that he had been a Pharisee and had hated the people who believed in Jesus. He had even put them into prison. Then Paul had seen a light from heaven and heard the Savior's voice. Now he believed in Jesus.

Acts 23:12–35; 25:13–23; 26:1–15

Paul testified to King Agrippa that the gospel was true. He said that Jesus had been resurrected. In a vision, Jesus Christ had told Paul to teach His gospel. Because Paul had obeyed, many people hated Paul.

Acts 26:16–23

King Agrippa said that Paul almost made him believe in Jesus. The king did not think Paul should be killed. But he had to send Paul to Rome, where Paul would be placed on trial.

Acts 26:27–32

Paul was in prison in Rome for two years. Many people came to see him. He taught them the gospel. Paul wrote letters to the Saints in other lands. Some of these letters, called epistles, are in the New Testament.

Acts 28:16–31

Paul knew he would be killed. He was not afraid. He had obeyed God's commandments. He had taught the gospel. He had finished his mission.

Paul knew that Heavenly Father loved him. He also knew that after he died, he would live with Heavenly Father and Jesus Christ.

2 Timothy 4:6–8

166

After the New Testament

Church leaders worked hard to teach people about Jesus Christ. They visited the Saints and wrote them letters. People joined the Church in many lands. Wicked people did not want people to believe in Jesus Christ.

Acts 6:2–4, 7; 11:19–21

Wicked people wanted to change the commandments. Some Saints listened to them. Many stopped believing in Jesus and did not obey His commandments.

Galatians 1:6–8; Titus 1:10–11; 1 John 2:18–19

167

The Apostles and many Saints were killed. No one was left to lead the Church. The keys of the priesthood were taken from the earth. The people did not have prophets to guide them. The Church of Jesus Christ was not on the earth anymore. The Apostles Peter and Paul had said this would happen.

Matthew 23:34; 24:8–10; Romans 8:36; 1 Corinthians 4:9–13; 1 Peter 4:12; Jesus the Christ, 745–46

Hundreds of years went by. There were many different churches. None of them had Apostles or the priesthood of God. None of the churches were the Church of Jesus Christ. But prophets had said that after many years the Church of Jesus Christ would return to the earth again.

Acts 3:19–26; 2 Thessalonians 2:1–4; 2 Timothy 4:3–4

In 1820 a boy named Joseph Smith wanted to know which church was the Church of Jesus Christ. He went into the woods near his home and prayed. He asked God to tell him which church was right.

Joseph Smith—History 1:3, 5, 10, 14–15

Heavenly Father and Jesus Christ came to Joseph Smith. The Savior told Joseph not to join any of the churches because none of them was His Church.

Joseph Smith—History 1:17–19

God chose to bring the Church of Jesus Christ back to the earth through Joseph Smith. God sent angels to give Joseph Smith the priesthood. He helped Joseph translate the Book of Mormon. On April 6, 1830, the Church of Jesus Christ was organized on the earth again.

Joseph Smith—History 1:33, 66–75

Just as Jesus chose Twelve Apostles when He was on the earth, God helped Joseph Smith choose Twelve Apostles to help him lead the Church. These men were given the power to teach the gospel and to do miracles.

Doctrine and Covenants 102:3; 107:22–23, 35

Jesus wants everyone to know about His Church. He told Joseph Smith to send missionaries to teach all people about The Church of Jesus Christ of Latter-day Saints.

Doctrine and Covenants 1:18, 30

The Church of Jesus Christ of Latter-day Saints is the same church that Jesus organized when He lived on the earth.

Doctrine and Covenants 115:4

Words to Know

altar   a sacred table-like structure in the temple when Jesus was alive. People offered sacrifices to God on the altar.

Angel   a heavenly messenger from God
Apostle   a leader in Jesus Christ's Church who testifies of Jesus Christ and teaches the gospel
authority   the right to use a power such as the priesthood or to have the right to punish those who don't obey the law

baptism [baptize]   an ordinance or ceremony in which a person with priesthood authority from God places another person entirely under water and lifts him or her back out. Baptism is required to become a member of Jesus Christ's Church. Also see *gift of the Holy Ghost.*

believe   to feel that something is right or true
betray   to turn against a friend or turn him or her over to an enemy
bless   to give good things or to help a person
blessing   a special prayer asking Heavenly Father to comfort or heal a person; the man who gives this prayer does so by the power of the priesthood which he holds. Any help we receive from God.
blind   unable to see

body of flesh and blood   the bodies that people on earth have that are made of skin, bones, muscles, and blood
bow [bowed]   to lower the head in respect

bridegroom   a man who is getting married
bury [buried]   to place the body of a dead person in a tomb or in the ground and cover with earth; to place something in the ground which a person wishes to hide

capture [captured]   to take a country or person by force
cave   an opening in a hillside

celebrate   to remember an important day by doing something special
choose   to pick or select
coin   a flat, metal piece of money

command   to tell someone or something what to do
commandment   something God tells people to do so they will be happy
counselor   a person who helps or gives advice to someone else

171

crown of thorns   sharp thorns arranged in a circle that was placed on Jesus's head

crucify   to kill a person by hanging him or her on a wooden cross as they did to Jesus Christ

deaf   not able to hear
desert   land that has very little water and few plants or animals
devil   another name for Satan
disciple   a person who believes in Jesus Christ and tries to be like Him
drown   to die from being underwater too long

earthquake   a strong shaking of the earth
eternal life   to become like our Father in Heaven and live with Him forever
everlasting   something that has no end; it goes on forever
evil   something that is bad and does not come from God

faith   to believe and trust in Jesus Christ
famine   a lack of food because not enough grows to feed everyone
fast   to go without food and water while seeking blessings from Heavenly Father
feast   a large meal usually eaten on a special day
filled with the Holy Ghost   to have the Holy Ghost fill a person's mind and heart with the truth
follow   to do what someone else does
forever   always
forgive   to stop being mad at someone who has done bad or harmful things

gift   a good thing God or others give to us
gift of the Holy Ghost   the right to have the Holy Ghost's help; it is given to a person after baptism by someone with priesthood authority

gospel   the teachings of Jesus Christ about how people should live so that they can return and live with Heavenly Father; it is Heavenly Father's plan of salvation
guard   a person who watches over people in prison; to watch over a person, place, or thing

heal   to make a sick or hurt person well
heaven   the place where Heavenly Father and Jesus Christ live
holy   something that is pure and clean and set apart for God's use
honeycomb   wax chambers made by bees. Bees fill these wax chambers with honey.

hymn   a church song or a song praising God

inn   a place where people can eat and sleep when they are on a journey
innkeeper   the person who runs an inn

join   to become part of a group

kingdom of God   the Church or the place where the righteous will live with Heavenly Father after this life
kneel [knelt]   to get down on your knees

lazy not willing to work

lead to guide others

leader a person who guides and is responsible for a group of people

leper a sick person with sores all over his or her body

lie to not tell the truth

loaf [loaves] the shape bread is baked in

locust a large flying insect sometimes used as food

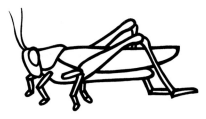

manger a box where food is put for animals to eat

member a person who belongs to a church or other group

miracle something unusual that happens because of the power of God

mission a special time of service to go and teach people the gospel of Jesus Christ and strengthen God's kingdom on earth

missionary a person who goes on a mission; sometimes the person is called to go to other lands

mock to make fun of

mount a mountain or large hill

neighbor someone living near your home; any other child of God

obey to do what has been asked or commanded

ordain men who hold priesthood authority lay their hands on another man's head to give him priesthood power and authority

organize to put in order Jesus Christ's Church

parable a story that teaches a principle or lesson

Passover a special celebration when Jewish people remember how God saved their people from the Egyptians at the time of Moses

peacemaker a person who helps people not to be angry with each other

power ability to do something. Also see *priesthood.*

praise to say good things about someone

pray to talk to God, giving Him thanks and asking for blessings

prayer what is said when a person prays

priest a leader in a church

priesthood the authority to act in God's name

prison a place where people who have broken the law are kept

produce to make or grow something

promise saying you will do something

prophet a person called by God to tell people what God wants them to do

repent to feel sorry for something you did and to promise never to do it again

resurrect to have our bodies and spirits come back together after we die

revelation something God tells His children

righteous obedient to God's commandments

robe   a long, flowing piece of clothing that is worn over other clothing

Sabbath   a special day of the week when people worship God by going to church and learning more about Him

sacrament   an ordinance in which bread and water are blessed and passed to members of the Church to remind them of Jesus Christ and to keep the commandments. The ordinance is done by men who have the priesthood.

sacred   anything given to us by God that is to be respected and reverenced

sacrifice   to give up something important for God or other people

Saint   a member of Jesus Christ's true Church

salvation   to be saved from sin and death so that we can live with Heavenly Father again

save   to rescue from danger. Jesus died to save us from physical death and the dangers of sin.

scriptures   books that contain the words of God given through His prophets

Second Coming   when Jesus will come to the earth again to save the righteous people and destroy the wicked

sermon   a talk given to a group of people about the gospel

servant   a person who serves or works for another person or for God

shepherd   a person who takes care of sheep

sin   to disobey Heavenly Father's commandments

sinner   a person who does not obey Heavenly Father's commandments

soldier   a person who carries out the orders of a king or ruler

sore   an area on the body that hurts or is bleeding

spirit   one of Heavenly Father's children who does not have a body of flesh and bones

steal   to take something that belongs to someone else

suffer   to feel great pain

synagogue   a building where Jewish people meet to worship God

tax   money people pay to the government

temple   God's house on the earth; a place to worship God; a holy place where sacred ordinances are performed

tempt   to try to get someone to do something that is wrong

testify   to tell other people that we know something is true

testimony   a feeling or thought from the Holy Ghost that the gospel is true

thief [thieves]   someone who steals from others

thorn   a sharp and pointed part of a plant that can hurt if touched

tithing   money given to God to build up His Church

tomb a place where dead people are buried

transfiguration a change in a person for a short period of time that makes it possible for him or her to be in the presence of Heavenly Father

translate to change words written or spoken in one language into words with the same meaning in a different language

travel to go from one place to another

trial an event at which people try to prove whether or not a person has broken the law

truth that which is true and right

vine the main stem of a plant, such as a grape, that has winding branches coming off of it. The vine keeps the branches alive.

vision a type of revelation from Heavenly Father

war a battle between enemies

wedding the event at which a man and a woman become married

whip a thin cord or rope; to use a whip to hit someone or something

wicked someone who is evil

widow a woman whose husband has died

wilderness a place where there are no towns or cities and few people live

wine a drink made from grapes

wise someone who is very smart and understands people, laws, and scriptures; also, someone who plans ahead

Wise Men men who came from the East to visit Jesus when He was a young child

worship to praise, love, and obey God

wound a bad injury to a person's body

Places to Know

(The numbers in parentheses are the chapters which tell about events that happened at these places.)

Map 1: The Holy Land in New Testament Times

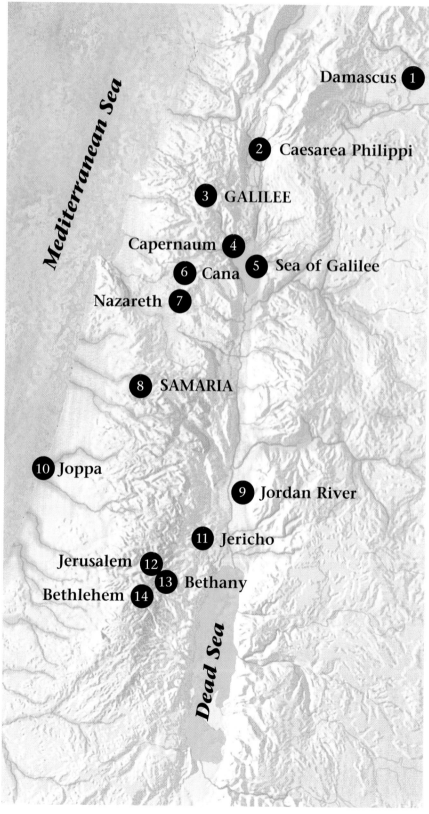

1. **Damascus** Paul was going to this city when Jesus appeared to him and told him to repent. (59)
2. **Caesarea Philippi** In this area Jesus testified of His death and Resurrection, and Peter testified that Jesus is the Son of God. (32)
3. **Galilee** Jesus spent a lot of time in this region teaching the gospel and healing the sick. (19–20, 34, 36)
4. **Capernaum** Jesus performed many miracles in this city. (23–25, 30)
5. **Sea of Galilee** Jesus taught the gospel to many people near here. Jesus calmed a storm and walked on the water of the Sea of Galilee. (18, 21, 29)
6. **Cana** Jesus turned water into wine at a wedding feast here. A man came here to ask Jesus to heal his sick son. (12, 16)
7. **Nazareth** Jesus grew up in this city. (2, 4, 9, 17)
8. **Samaria** Jesus taught a woman about living water at a well in this land. Most Jews hated the people of Samaria. (15, 58)
9. **Jordan River** John the Baptist baptized Jesus Christ in this river. (10)
10. **Joppa** Peter brought Tabitha back to life here. (60)
11. **Jericho** In the parable of the good Samaritan, a man was nearly killed while traveling on the road to this city. (35)
12. **Jerusalem** Jesus and His Apostles spent a lot of time teaching in this city. Jesus died and was resurrected here. (6, 39–40, 44–57, 63) See Map 2 for additional stories that occurred in Jerusalem.
13. **Bethany** Lazarus, whom Jesus raised from the dead, lived here with his sisters Mary and Martha. (43)
14. **Bethlehem** Jesus Christ was born here. (5, 7)

Map 2: Jerusalem at the Time of Jesus

1. **Golgotha** This may be where Jesus Christ died on the cross. (53)
2. **Garden Tomb** This may be where Jesus Christ was buried, was resurrected, and talked with Mary Magdalene. (53, 54)
3. **Pool of Bethesda** Jesus healed a man on the Sabbath here. (27)
4. **Temple** Here the angel Gabriel promised Zacharias that he would have a son, who was John the Baptist. Jesus taught at this temple. He also drove people out of the temple who were selling animals for sacrifices. (1, 6, 9, 11, 13, 45, 56)
5. **Garden of Gethsemane** Jesus Christ prayed, suffered for our sins, was betrayed by Judas Iscariot, and was arrested in this garden. (51, 52)
6. **Mount of Olives** Jesus taught about His Second Coming here. (46)
7. **House of Caiaphas** This may be the place where Jewish leaders put Jesus on trial, accusing Him of breaking the law. (52)
8. **Upper Room** The room where Jesus and His Apostles ate the Passover was probably in this area. Jesus taught His Apostles about the sacrament shortly before going to the Garden of Gethsemane. (49, 50)

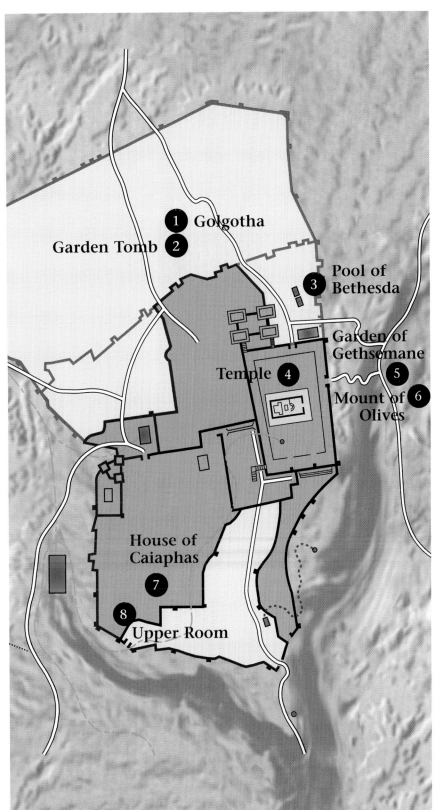

Other Places to Know

America   Jesus Christ visited the people in the Americas after His Resurrection and taught them the gospel. He called twelve disciples to lead the Church here. (40)

Earth   the planet where we all live. Jesus Christ made the earth for us. (Introduction)

Egypt   a country south of the Holy Land. Joseph was told by an angel to take his family to Egypt so that Herod would not kill the baby Jesus. (8)

Heaven   the place where Heavenly Father lives. (Introduction)

Holy Land   the land where Jesus lived and taught. Judea, Samaria, and Galilee are all in the Holy Land. (Introduction)

Rome   the capital city of the Roman Empire. Paul taught the gospel while he was in prison in Rome. (63)

People to Know

Agrippa   a Roman king who ruled in Israel. Paul told Agrippa about Jesus Christ.

Ananias   a disciple of Jesus Christ who lived in Damascus. He blessed Paul and took care of him after Paul was blinded during a vision.

Anna   a faithful widow who saw Jesus when He was a baby and taught people that Jesus was the Son of God and the Redeemer

Caiaphas   the Jewish high priest who took part in condemning Jesus at His trial

Elias   an Old Testament prophet

Elisabeth   the mother of John the Baptist

Gabriel   the angel who visited Mary and told her that she would be the mother of Jesus. Gabriel also came to Zacharias and told him he would have a son who would be John the Baptist.

God   may refer to Heavenly Father or to Jesus Christ

Heavenly Father   the Father of our spirit bodies. We pray to Him.

Herod   a wicked king who ruled in Jerusalem when Jesus was born. He had all the babies in Bethlehem killed in hopes of killing the baby Jesus.

Holy Ghost   one of the three members of the Godhead. He helps Jesus Christ and Heavenly Father. He has power to help people know the truth. He is a spirit and does not have a body of flesh and bone.

Isaiah   an Old Testament prophet who wrote about Jesus

Jairus   a Jewish leader in Capernaum. Jesus raised his daughter from the dead.

James   one of Jesus's Twelve Apostles. He was one of Peter's counselors after Jesus's death.

Jesus Christ   the Son of God and Savior of the world. He suffered and died for our sins.

Jews   Israelites who were part of the kingdom of Judah. Jesus was a Jew.

John   one of Jesus's Twelve Apostles. He was one of Peter's counselors after Jesus's death.

John the Baptist   the prophet who baptized Jesus. He was the son of Zacharias and Elisabeth.

Joseph   Mary's husband. Joseph took good care of Jesus and Mary.

Joseph Smith   When Joseph Smith was a boy, Heavenly Father and Jesus Christ visited him. They told him not to join any of the churches then on the earth because they had all strayed from the truth. Through Joseph Smith, the true Church of Jesus Christ was restored to the earth.

Judas Iscariot   one of Jesus's Apostles. Judas turned Jesus over to wicked men for 30 pieces of silver.

Lazarus   a man Jesus raised from the dead

Mary   the mother of Jesus

Mary and Martha   the sisters of Lazarus and friends of Jesus

Mary Magdalene   Jesus's friend and the first person to see Jesus after His Resurrection

Matthias   a disciple of Jesus who was called to take Judas Iscariot's place as one of the Twelve Apostles

Messiah   another name for Jesus Christ

Moses   an Old Testament prophet

Nicodemus   a ruler of the Jews who believed that Jesus was the Savior. Jesus taught Nicodemus about baptism.

Paul   a man who did not like Jesus's disciples until he saw Jesus in a vision and became converted. He then served God and became one of the Apostles. He was also known as Saul.

Peter   one of Jesus's Twelve Apostles and President of the Church after Jesus's death

Pharisees   leaders of the Jews. Most of them hated Jesus and His disciples.

Pontius Pilate   the Roman governor in Jerusalem. The Jews told Pilate to crucify Jesus, and Pilate allowed Jesus to be killed.

Romans   the people who controlled the land Jesus lived in during His life

Samaritans   a group of people who lived in the land Jesus lived in. The Jews and Samaritans usually did not like each other.

Satan   a spirit son of Heavenly Father. He did not obey Heavenly Father, so he was sent out of heaven. He became the devil. Satan tries to tempt people to do that which is wrong.

Saul   see *Paul*

Savior   Jesus Christ is the Savior. He suffered and died for our sins. Because of Him, we can be forgiven of our sins, if we repent, and we will live forever.

Silas   a missionary and Paul's friend

Simeon   a righteous man who saw the baby Jesus at the temple in Jerusalem

Simon   a man in Samaria. He tried to buy the priesthood from Peter and John. They taught him that a person cannot buy the priesthood.

Stephen   a righteous leader of the Church of Jesus Christ. The Pharisees killed him.

Tabitha   a good woman whom Peter brought back to life

Zacharias   the father of John the Baptist

Photographs of the Holy Land

(Numbers in parentheses are the chapter numbers of stories that took place at or near the place pictured.)

Bethlehem Jesus Christ was born in this city. (5, 7)

Temple This is a model of the temple in Jerusalem where Jesus taught the gospel and drove out the people who sold animals for sacrifices. (1, 6, 9, 11, 13, 45, 56)

Steps to the Temple These are the actual steps that led to the temple.

Nazareth Jesus grew up in this city. (2, 4, 9, 17)

Jerusalem Jesus and His Apostles spent a lot of time teaching in this city. Jesus died and was resurrected here. (6, 39–40, 44–57, 63)

Jordan River John the Baptist baptized Jesus Christ somewhere in this river. (10)

Judean Wilderness Jesus Christ fasted and was tempted by the devil in the wilderness after His baptism. (11)

Samaria Jesus taught a woman about living water at a well in this land. Most Jews hated the people of Samaria. (15, 58)

Galilee and the Sea of Galilee Many people believe this hillside is where Jesus gave the Sermon on the Mount. The Sea of Galilee is in the background. Jesus taught the gospel to many people, including His Apostles, near here. Jesus calmed a storm on the Sea of Galilee. (18–22, 29, 34, 36)

Capernaum These ruins are in the city of Capernaum. Jesus performed many miracles in this city. (23–25, 30)

Caesarea Philippi In this area Jesus testified of His death and Resurrection, and Peter testified that Jesus is the Son of God. (32)

Jericho In the parable of the good Samaritan, a man was nearly killed while traveling on the road to this city. (35)

Mount Tabor This may be where the Transfiguration of Jesus Christ took place. (33)

Garden of Gethsemane Jesus Christ prayed, suffered for our sins, was betrayed by Judas Iscariot, and was arrested in this garden. (51, 52)

Golgotha This may be where Jesus Christ died on the cross. (53)

Garden Tomb This may be where Jesus Christ was buried, was resurrected, and talked with Mary Magdalene. (53, 54)

New Testament Time Line

Before Jesus's Birth to A.D. 2	A.D. 11	A.D. 31	A.D. 32
1 Elisabeth and Zacharias 2 Mary and the Angel 3 John the Baptist Is Born 4 Joseph and the Angel (A.D. 0–2) 5 Jesus Christ Is Born 6 Presentation at the Temple 7 The Wise Men 8 Wicked King Herod	9 The Boy Jesus	10 Jesus Is Baptized 11 Jesus Is Tempted 12 The Wedding in Cana 13 Jesus and His Heavenly Father's House 14 Nicodemus 15 The Woman at the Well 16 The Leader's Son 17 Angry People in Nazareth 18 Jesus Chooses His Apostles 19 The Sermon on the Mount 20 Jesus Teaches about Prayer 21 Jesus Commands the Winds and the Waves 22 The Man with the Evil Spirits 23 The Man Who Could Not Walk	24 Jairus's Daughter Is Raised from the Dead 25 A Woman Touches Jesus's Clothes 26 Jesus Forgives a Woman 27 Doing His Father's Work on Earth

The number before a title indicates the chapter of this book where you can read the story.

A.D. 33	A.D. 34	Last Week of the Savior's Life	A.D. 34–70

28 Jesus Feeds 5,000 People

29 Jesus Walks on the Water

30 The Bread of Life

31 Jesus Heals a Deaf Man

32 Peter Testifies of Christ

33 Appearing in Glory: The Transfiguration

34 The Boy with an Evil Spirit

35 The Good Samaritan

36 Jesus Tells Three Parables

The Lost Sheep

The Lost Coin

The Lost Son

37 The Ten Lepers

38 The Pharisee and the Publican

39 Jesus Heals a Blind Man

40 The Good Shepherd

41 Jesus Blesses the Children

42 The Rich Young Man

43 Jesus Brings Lazarus Back to Life

44 The Savior Goes to Jerusalem

45 The Widow's Mites

46 The Second Coming

47 The Ten Virgins

48 The Talents

49 The First Sacrament

50 Other Teachings at the Last Supper

51 Jesus Suffers in the Garden of Gethsemane

52 The Trials of Jesus

53 Jesus Is Crucified

54 Jesus Is Risen

55 The Apostles Lead the Church

56 Peter Heals a Man

57 Wicked Men Kill Stephen

58 Simon and the Priesthood

59 Saul Learns about Jesus

60 Peter Brings Tabitha Back to Life

61 Paul and Silas in Prison

62 Paul Obeys the Holy Ghost

63 Paul Finishes His Mission

Dates and order of events are approximate.